STALKING

LAURA LA BELLA

ROSEN
PUBLISHING®

New York

Published in 2016 by The Rosen Publishing Group, Inc.
29 East 21st Street, New York, NY 10010

Library of Congress Cataloging-in-Publication Data

La Bella, Laura.
Stalking/Laura La Bella.
    pages cm.—(Confronting violence against women)
Includes bibliographical references and index.
ISBN 978-1-4994-6046-9 (library bound)—ISBN 978-1-4994-6047-6 (pbk.)—
ISBN 978-1-4994-6048-3 (6-pack)
1. Stalking—Juvenile literature. 2. Stalking victims—Juvenile literature.
3. Stalking—Law and legislation. I. Title.
HV6594.L3 2016
364.15'8—dc23

                                         2014048192

Manufactured in the United States of America

CONTENTS

INTRODUCTION

Olympic gold medal gymnast Shawn Johnson was a celebrity competitor on the television dance competition *Dancing with the Stars* in 2009, when she was seventeen. Johnson and her family found out about a stalker named Robert O'Ryan, who said he was going to travel to Los Angeles, California, where the show is produced, to see Johnson. He claimed he was going to marry Johnson and that she was the mother of his unborn children. Johnson and her family decided to alter her normal routine so O'Ryan would have difficulty contacting her if he arrived in Los Angeles. Johnson drove to and from the television studio in different vehicles, changed hotels frequently, and cancelled all of her personal appearances and interviews. Johnson's family also employed a bodyguard to accompany Johnson whenever she went out.

On March 23, 2009, O'Ryan arrived at the ABC Studios lot where *Dancing with the Stars* is produced. He was arrested when he jumped a fence surrounding the property. Police searched O'Ryan's car and found two loaded guns, duct tape, a wooden club, gifts, and handwritten letters and poetry addressed to Johnson. In one of the letters, O'Ryan wrote, "No matter what happens I will always love you."

While competing on ABC's *Dancing with the Stars*, Shawn Johnson, an Olympic gold medalist, became the victim of a stalker. She later testified against him during his trial.

Johnson testified at O'Ryan's trial, where she told prosecutors that she did not know O'Ryan and that she was fearful for her life. After learning of his obsession, Johnson told the court she considered quitting *Dancing with the Stars* and returning home to Iowa. Johnson was scared to face her stalker in person, but during an interview on *Good Morning America*, a national morning news show, she said, "I had to stand up for everybody else out there that's been through it ... I just had to go there and kind of help put him away."

O'Ryan was found guilty of felony stalking and burglary and two misdemeanors for concealed weapon violations. He was also ordered to go through a mental evaluation. He was later sentenced to five years in a mental hospital.

More than six million people in the United States are stalked each year. According to the National Center for Victims of Crime, 66 percent of stalking victims are women. Stalkers can target people they know, such as ex-girlfriends or ex-boyfriends, or people they have never met, such as celebrities or other public figures. With the growing use of social media and the Internet, stalkers can easily find out where you live, where you spend your time, who your friends are, and the places you like to go.

If you think you are being stalked, learning how to protect yourself and keep yourself safe are vitally important. Document your stalker's behavior, limit the personal information you share on social media, avoid going to places alone, and tell friends and family about any harassment that happens. Stalking is a serious crime, and you should take any form of harassment or threatening behavior seriously. Any and all stalking incidents should be reported to law enforcement. By understanding what stalking is and how stalkers work, you can begin to protect yourself from the fear, anxiety, and uncertainty of being stalked.

CHAPTER 1

What Is Stalking?

Kate Brennan has spent more than ten years as the victim of a stalker. In a memoir titled *In His Sights*, Brennan outlines the torment she has experienced at the hands of a former boyfriend who will not leave her alone.

Brennan, which is not her real name, first met "Paul," a freelance photographer, at a party. They began to date and eventually moved in together. After Paul's behavior became erratic, Brennan ended the relationship and moved out. At first, Paul called her repeatedly, drove by her house, and cancelled her mail-forwarding order so her mail continued to arrive at his home. Soon, Paul stopped contacting her directly. In an interview with the *New York Times* to promote her book, Brennan detailed how his stalking became creative and deeply unsettling. She told the newspaper that Paul's friends would call her to tell her Paul had seen her out the day before. Strangers, who she suspects were hired by Paul, would approach her to tell her she was being watched. Numerous times Brennan changed the locks on her apartment, but her residence would consistently be broken into and small items would be rearranged. She'd find a kitchen spoon lying on her bed or a bar of soap from a bathroom on the kitchen counter. These small gestures by Paul were meant to let her know he was there and he could get to her.

After Paul and his new wife bought the house across the street from Brennan's apartment, she finally moved. She repeatedly involved local law enforcement, but with no direct threats to her life

Stalking can take on many forms, from unwanted letters and gifts to constant phone calls to break-ins at your home.

and no direct way to prove the harassment was coming from Paul, police were limited in what they could do.

Brennan decided to tell her story to help give a voice to the millions of women who are stalked each year. To protect herself, she wrote her story using a fake name and altered physical descriptions of Paul and other people in her life to protect their identities. She did not, however, change details of the events that took place. Brennan told the *New York Times*, "I think it's a game for him … Much more fun to just mess with me and spoil my life in this way and constantly remind me I can't get rid of him, that he's got control over me." She said her only hope is to outlive her stalker. "The only way that I'll know the stalking will stop is if he's dead."

Brennan's decade of being stalked has disrupted her life, has caused her to move, has left her feeling helpless, and has her living in a constant state of fear.

Defining Stalking

Stalking is defined as any behavior directed at a specific person with the intent to cause fear. According to the National Center for Victims of Crime, 6.6 million people are stalked every year in the United States. The majority of these victims are stalked by someone they know. Sixty-six percent of female victims and 41 percent of male victims are stalked by a current or former intimate partner. Also, 46 percent of victims experience at least one unwanted contact from their stalker per week, and 11 percent of victims are stalked for more than five years. Women between the ages of eighteen and twenty-four experience the highest rate of stalking.

Stalking is a prevalent problem for women. One in six women has experienced stalking at some point in her life. Teenagers are not immune to being stalked. Roughly one in five female victims of stalking is between the ages of eleven and seventeen.

Unfortunately, stalkers can be anyone. An ex-boyfriend, an ex-husband, or a friend can stalk you. You can be stalked by someone you've never met before. Most commonly, stalkers are individuals with whom you've had some sort of relationship. Most stalking cases involve men stalking women. However, anyone can be stalked by anyone else. It's not uncommon for men to stalk other men, women to stalk other women, or women to stalk men.

A Stalker's Behavior

A stalker's irregular, unpredictable, and odd behavior is what causes fear in his or her victims. For a stalker it's about control and power over the victim. The majority of stalkers, more than two-thirds, pursue their victims at least once per week, and three-fourths use more than one method of contact. Some stalkers engage in daily contact with their victims.

Stalkers engage in a wide range of behaviors meant to intimidate and instill fear in their victims. Context, or the circumstances in which behaviors or actions take place, is critical in understanding stalking behavior. Many behaviors—repeated phone calls, unwanted contact, being followed—are not criminal acts in and of

Many people associate being followed with stalking. But there are many ways stalkers can intimidate their victims.

themselves, but collectively they can be viewed by you and law enforcement as threatening behavior or harassment.

Stalkers engage in a wide range of behaviors that may or may not include explicit threats to your safety. These behaviors can include:

- Following you and showing up wherever you are
- Sending you unwanted gifts, letters, cards, text messages, or e-mails
- Repeatedly contacting you or harassing you via phone call, text, social media, letters, or e-mail
- Damaging or vandalizing your home, car, or other property
- Monitoring your phone calls, activity on social media, or computer use
- Using technology, such as hidden cameras or Global Positioning System (GPS), to track where you go, whom you are with, and what you are doing
- Driving by or hanging out at your home, school, or work
- Threatening to hurt you, your family, your friends, or your pets
- Finding information about you by using public records or online search services, hiring investigators, going through your garbage, or contacting friends, family, neighbors, or coworkers
- Posting information or spreading rumors about you on the Internet, in a public place, or by word of mouth

Technology and Stalking

A quick birthday text message, posting family photos of special events to social media, or using status updates to announce personal news like your new relationship ... modern technology has given us immeasurable ways to stay in contact with one another

THE DIFFERENCE BETWEEN STALKING AND HARASSMENT

Stalking and harassment are both crimes, but these two forms of unwanted contact are very different in the eyes of the law.

Stalking is when one person performs a series of acts over a period of time that cause another person to feel intimidated, frightened, terrorized, or fearful for his or her safety and the safety of family, friends, or household pets. These individual acts are not necessarily crimes by themselves, but grouped together to show a pattern of behavior, they constitute stalking.

Harassment is when one person fears being injured or harmed by another person. It can involve direct or indirect threats of injury or death.

With stalking, often two or more acts need to be committed for law enforcement to intervene in some way. With harassment, one threat made knowingly, or even a threat of something happening in the future, can result in a person being arrested and charged with the crime of harassment.

and share our lives with friends and family. Social media has also made it easier to be stalked.

Stalkers are skilled at using social media to watch your every move and to stalk you in new, more public ways. Stalkers can use social media to post personal information, such as your phone numbers and addresses, online; verbally attack or threaten you;

New York State Senator Tim Kennedy supported Jackie's Law, which made it a felony to install a GPS tracking device with the intent to stalk. Jackie Wisniewski was murdered by her boyfriend, who tracked her whereabouts with a GPS he installed in her car.

and follow your life by monitoring your posts to find out where you are, who you are with, and who your friends are.

Other uses of modern technology, such as GPS, enable a stalker to track your movements, for instance by hiding a smartphone in your car. Spyware software, which can be installed on your home computer or even sent through e-mail, can enable a stalker to track your online activity. Spyware is designed to send its owner a copy of every task you perform on your computer, from each keystroke you make, including your passwords, to every website you visit and every e-mail you send and receive. Spyware is very difficult to detect on a computer, so many stalking victims aren't even aware that their computer use is being monitored.

If you're being stalked, or suspect that you might be, you can protect your online presence by either avoiding social media altogether or by employing a number of precautions to make it difficult for someone to learn information about you.

Make your social media profiles private, enabling only well-known friends and family to see status updates or posts. Avoid tagging photos with information about where you are and whom you are with. If someone else tags you in a photo, it can be visible to stalkers who may be friends with or have access to the

Social media makes it possible for people to know what you are doing, when you are doing it, and with whom. For stalkers, it's an easy way to follow your behavior and gather information about you.

other person's page. To block this, change your privacy settings so you have to authorize a tag before it appears on your, or anyone else's, page.

Vary your username so all of your social media accounts use different names. Using the same username might make it easier for friends and family to find you, but it also makes it easier for stalkers to locate you, too. Only friend people you know, and avoid friending anyone you think may be stalking you or may be friends with your stalker.

Report suspicious or threatening behavior immediately. If someone posts unwanted or threatening messages to your social media pages, capture an image of the threat for law enforcement, then block the person, withdraw from social media, or close your accounts.

Protect your privacy by making it difficult for your stalker to find information about you. Some victims even go so far as to make sure no records have their full name or address on them. This includes their driver's license, car registration, doctor's offices, magazine subscriptions, business cards, mail order companies, credit cards, their school or their children's school, all bills, and any stores they visit that keep personal information on file, such as a dry cleaner or the pharmacy.

By controlling or eliminating what you post online about yourself, your interests, where you spend your time, and with whom you spend it, you can take some power away from your stalker.

CHAPTER 2

Why Does Stalking Happen?

One of the most recent, highly publicized cases of stalking involved a woman named Jodi Arias and her on-again, off-again boyfriend, Travis Alexander. Arias and Alexander had a tumultuous relationship. Their relationship turned into a mutual obsession with one another that included jealousy, lies, stalking, and, finally, Alexander's murder.

On June 9, 2008, friends found Alexander's body on the floor of his shower. His throat had been slit, he had nearly thirty stab wounds, and he had been shot in the head. Arias was arrested and charged with first-degree murder.

During the course of the trial, Arias testified that Alexander hit and threatened her and pressured her to engage in a variety of unsavory sexual situations. Alexander's friends testified that Arias was stalking Alexander. She hacked into his computer and e-mail, slit his tires, climbed through the dog door of his home and was found hiding in his closet, and followed him on dates with other women. In testimony, Arias confessed to killing Alexander in self-defense after Alexander attacked her. At the conclusion of the trial, Arias was convicted of first-degree murder, which is defined as premeditated and willful or intentional.

Who Stalks?

It's common to think that most stalking incidents are done by men and women who stalk someone they used to date or someone they have a romantic obsession with. But in reality, a person can be stalked by anyone for any reason. According to the Network of Victim Assistance:

- Eighty-three percent of female victims are stalked by men.
- Forty-four percent of male victims are stalked by men.
- Eight percent of female victims are stalked by women.
- Forty-seven percent of male victims are stalked by women.
- Recidivism, or a relapse in a certain type of behavior, occurs in more than 60 percent of stalking cases.

While both men and women can be stalkers, each gender's approach to stalking is different. Female stalkers rarely use third parties, or other people, to deliver messages. They are more likely to write letters, text, or send unwanted gifts; less likely to make personal contact with their victim; and more likely to leave messages that contain unwanted declarations of love or of wanting to be with the

Making personal and frequent contact with their victims is how stalkers intimidate and instill fear. Contact can come in many different forms, including letters, gifts, texts, phone calls, and third parties.

MYTHS and *FACTS*

MYTH Stalking is limited to following someone around and contacting him or her obsessively.

FACT One in four stalking victims reports being stalked through some form of technology, including e-mail, instant messaging, social media, or computer hacking. Others report being monitored by GPS, video or digital cameras, and listening devices.

MYTH Stalking isn't a big deal.

FACT Stalking can disrupt one's life in immeasurable ways. Victims can experience anxiety, insomnia, distress, and severe depression from constantly living in fear or worrying about the uncertainty of when their stalker might strike again. Some stalking victims have been forced to leave their jobs or move to get away from their stalker.

MYTH If you ignore a stalker, he or she will just go away.

FACT Stalkers rarely decide to stop stalking without some sort of intervention. Most stalking behaviors escalate to force a reaction from the victim or to increase the stalker's feeling of power and control over the victim.

person they are stalking. They are more likely to threaten their victim's friends or family. If they had a previous intimate relationship with their victim, they are more likely to be violent.

Male stalkers are more likely to be violent toward the victim and often directly or indirectly threaten violence. They are more likely to damage property, break into their victim's home, and be threatening in their messages. They are also more likely to use third parties to deliver threatening messages or drop off unwanted gifts.

Types of Stalkers

Not all stalkers are the same, nor do they stalk for the same reasons. While there are no set definitions for types of stalking, there are some general categories that most stalkers fit into. The National Center for Victims of Crimes (NCVC) and the Stalking Resource Center, a program of the NCVC, have created categories to help better define the various types of stalking. It's important to note that not all stalkers fit into these categories and that these groupings represent generalizations about some of the most common types of stalking and motivations.

The *rejected stalker* is someone who begins pursuing a former romantic partner after a breakup. The stalker wants to be in the relationship again or is seeking revenge for being hurt or rejected by the victim. The rejected stalker is likely to intimidate his or her victim, and the stalking tends to be persistent and intrusive. It's not uncommon for the stalker and the victim to have had a tumultuous relationship where violence or dating abuse has occurred. This type of stalker is the most resistant to efforts and interventions aimed at ending the stalking behavior. Intimate partner stalkers are also more likely to physically approach the victim with a weapon.

The *resentful stalker* is motivated to frighten, intimidate, or cause

There are many different types of stalkers and many reasons why people stalk. But it's commonly recognized that stalking in general is done to instill fear and to intimidate one's victim.

distress with the purpose of getting revenge for being hurt, upset, or humiliated by the victim. Many resentful stalkers are irrationally paranoid. These stalkers may or may not know their victims personally. They can be the most obsessive in their pursuit of a victim and are most likely to be verbally abusive or threatening. However, they are one of the least likely to engage in physical assault.

The *predatory stalker* stalks his or her victims as part of a plan to attack them. The most common type of assault used by the predatory stalker is sexual assault. Often, this stalker is motivated by the

Stalking creates uncertainly in the victim, who is constantly uneasy about whether the stalker is watching or following him or her.

promise or idea of sexual gratification and power and control over the victim. Many predatory stalkers do not contact their victims during their stalking and instead engage in surveillance, voyeurism, and exhibitionism. These stalkers have a higher potential to become physically violent with their victims.

The *intimacy seeker* wants to establish an intimate, loving relationship with the victim and may believe that the victim is in love with him or her. Intimacy stalkers are often delusional, which is a mental illness in which a person believes something to be true without plausible evidence. The intimacy stalker interprets responses from the victim, even negative ones, as further encouragement. This type of stalker's behavior and beliefs about a person are often very difficult to change or alter. The stalker is undeterred by legal interventions and sees protective orders or arrests as a challenge to prove his or her love to the victim. If the stalker realizes he or she is being rejected, he or she could become threatening or violent toward the victim. Most commonly, these stalkers write letters; obsessively call, text, or leave messages; and send gifts to their victims.

CHAPTER 3

How to Cope with Being Stalked

For Hannah Perryman, four years of being stalked started in 2004 when she was in fifth grade. While attending a sleepover, Hannah was assaulted by a girl who lived in her neighborhood in Illinois. The girl was arrested and ordered to undergo counseling. A few months after the assault took place, the girl started showing up in front of Hannah's home and riding her bike or pacing in front of the house for several minutes each day. The stalking began to escalate with the girl spending hours outside the Perryman home. Hannah's family reported the behavior to police, but the police could not do anything to help. The girl wasn't breaking any laws by loitering outside the home. Hannah began to have nightmares and withdrew from her friends.

One day Hannah and her family were outside doing yard work when the girl rode her bicycle nearby and threatened Hannah. The Perryman family immediately called the police. But Illinois state stalking laws require two documented incidents before charges can be filed against a stalker. Nearly a year later, the girl threatened Hannah again, and prosecutors were finally able to charge the girl with stalking, which is a felony crime in Illinois.

Stalking Can Disrupt Your Life

If you are being stalked, you may feel a wide range of emotions as a result of not knowing what will happen next, and when. The effects of stalking can impact your mental and physical well-being, as well as your social life at work and school, and even your finances. You may experience:

• Denial, confusion, and self-doubt about what is happening. You may also wonder if you are overreacting.

Stalking can cause disruption in your life. Filing police reports takes time away from school, work, and your family, and it can be expensive if stalking forces you to move, hire an attorney, or install safety measures around your home.

- Frustration if little can be done to stop your stalker's behavior.
- Guilt, embarrassment, shame, or self-blame for feeling like you have unknowingly caused the stalking or for the perception by others that you may have encouraged your stalker.
- Fear of being alone, of being hurt, or of family, friends, and pets being injured by your stalker.
- Feelings of isolation because you are afraid to leave the house.
- Trouble concentrating at work or in school or a decrease in performance at work or school.
- Nightmares or trouble falling asleep.
- Becoming more suspicious of others and their motives.
- A dependency on alcohol or drugs to self-medicate.
- Physical ailments such as headaches, high blood pressure, or other stress-related medical problems.
- The exacerbation of existing conditions, such as asthma, high blood pressure, sleeping issues, and other ailments.
- Being forced to find other employment if the stalking interrupts your work.
- Being forced to leave or switch schools if the stalking impacts your ability to attend class or complete assignments.
- Negative impact on your social relationships, including current partners, friends, and family.
- Avoiding social interactions where your stalker might show up.
- Loss of wages because you left work or were forced to quit your job.
- Financial drain from expenses related to stalking, such as relocating, legal costs, repairing property damage, and medical treatment.

Protecting Yourself from a Former Partner

Many stalking victims know their stalkers. Sometimes a former romantic partner takes a breakup particularly badly and retaliates by trying to disrupt your life. If you think you are being stalked by someone you were in a relationship with, you need to take steps to protect yourself. Try to end the relationship together with the help of a counselor, in as peaceful a way as possible. A counselor can help both of you work through your feelings and provide alternative ways of managing feelings of rejection, anger, resentment, and revenge. A counselor may suggest that you and your former partner take some time where you both refrain from contacting one another. This gives you both a chance to calm down, adjust to the breakup, and begin moving on. During this time, you should avoid talking to mutual friends about your relationship. You don't want any negative comments you say to make their way back to your

There are ways to deal with being stalked, from professional counseling and police involvement to making a list of all the instances, real and perceived, of your being stalked.

former partner. You should also avoid going to places where he or she normally shops, hangs out, or eats.

Many times in a relationship, we share our personal information, such as passwords to our online accounts, banking information such as account numbers, and keys to our home or apartment. To further protect yourself, you should consider changing all passwords, creating new usernames, changing all personal identification numbers (PINs), requesting new bank accounts, and changing all locks on your doors.

Ending a relationship can also produce conflicting emotions. You may still feel attracted to the person, but you may be angry. You may feel bad for hurting this person, so you appear excessively nice when you see him or her. These mixed messages can be confusing for him or her and may incite feelings of anger and resentment, which could lead to stalking behavior. Avoid sending mixed messages to your former partner. There must be no contact of any kind under any circumstances if you think you are being stalked. You should also avoid dating your former partner's friends. By giving this person few, if any, reasons to think about you, you can help lessen the chance of being stalked by a former partner. If you have already received a protective order against your former partner, you should never knowingly place yourself within close proximity to him or her or do anything that could be viewed as encouraging contact of any kind.

When You Don't Know Your Stalker

It's possible to be stalked by someone you don't know. Roughly 10 percent of stalking victims are stalked by a stranger with whom they have had no previous relationship. Stranger stalking, where the stalker and victim do not know one another at all, most often happens to celebrities, television personalities, politicians, or other public figures. It may be rare, but it does happen to noncelebrities.

Commonly, people who stalk someone they do not know often have an emotional disturbance that leads them to believe the person they are stalking is in love with them, is supposed to be with them romantically, or is communicating with them in some way, such as in celebrity interviews or via telepathy.

If you feel you are being stalked and you cannot identify the individual, take steps to protect yourself. Most anonymous stalking happens via the Internet, where a wealth of information can be found on nearly anyone. Every post you make, photo you share, or comment you write has the potential to offer information about you to your stalker. Increase your privacy settings on your social media accounts, allow only people you know well to have access to your posts and photos, and be judicial about what you choose to share online. To avoid offering any information at all, avoid social media altogether.

Coping with Being Stalked

Stalking is serious behavior that should never be ignored. Over time, stalking not only disrupts your life, but it can also lead to violence, assault, or murder. Stalking behaviors should be taken seriously as soon as they begin.

If you think you are being stalked, contact your local law enforcement agency immediately to report what is happening. You may not yet have any physical evidence of being stalked, but making them aware of what's happening is an important first step. You should:

Trust your instincts: It's easy to ignore small signs that something is wrong or when a former romantic partner is acting out because of a breakup. But calling you multiple times a day, leaving unwanted or threatening messages on your social media accounts, driving by your home, and following you around are not normal behaviors. If you feel unsafe, you probably are.

Avoid communication with your stalker: Under no circumstances should you engage your stalker. Even telling your stalker to leave you alone or go away may be encouraging the behavior. Some stalkers feel emboldened by any reactions they cause in their victims. Don't give a stalker any reason to think you enjoy or are encouraging what he or she is doing.

Involving the police as soon as you realize you are being stalked is a smart move to make. By having an official record on hand with law enforcement of each instance of stalking, you can build a case against your stalker.

Take all threats seriously: If your stalker threatens violence, don't ignore it as the empty threats of an angry ex-partner or ex-friend. Call the police immediately. Stalkers who threaten violence are among the most dangerous and are more likely to carry out their threats.

Keep all evidence and document all interactions: Write down each and every time your stalker follows you, sends you messages or gifts, shows up at your job or school, threatens you, threatens your family or friends, breaks into your home, or damages your property. In addition, keep all items your stalker sends to you, including all gifts and messages. These items may be used later to help prove to a court of law that you are being stalked or that you fear for your safety.

Contact a crisis hotline: Staffed by highly trained professionals, crisis hotlines can provide you with valuable information on ways to protect yourself, as well as legal protections you are entitled to. Crisis counselors can also give you advice about ways to protect yourself, to increase your privacy, and to manage your feelings of fear, intimidation, and helplessness.

10 GREAT QUESTIONS TO ASK WHEN YOU'RE ASKING FOR HELP

1. How do I know I'm being stalked?

2. What is the difference between stalking and being pursued romantically?

3. What are my legal rights and protections?

4. Should I confront my stalker and find out what he or she wants?

5. How do I protect my children, my family, and my friends?

6. What is a protection order, and can it help me?

7. What protections can law enforcement agencies provide?

8. How do I get my stalker to stop harassing me?

9. What is cyberstalking?

10. Is stalking different from being bullied?

CHAPTER 4

Stalking and the Law

In 1989, at the age of twenty-one, Rebecca Schaeffer was a successful model and television actress. She was the star of the CBS comedy *My Sister Sam* and had completed a series of promising roles in several major films.

A nineteen-year-old man named Robert John Bardo became fascinated with Schaeffer. He built a shrine to her in his home and twice traveled to Los Angeles, California, where Schaeffer's television show was produced. Both times he was denied access to the studio lot by security. Undeterred, Bardo hired a private detective, who discovered Schaeffer's address through the California Department of Motor Vehicles (DMV) and used various other computer databases to learn what kind of car Schaeffer drove, the people she called on her phone, and where she liked to shop and spend her time. Bardo traveled to Los Angeles again, this time going to her apartment building. After Schaeffer answered the door and asked Bardo to leave, he waited, then rang her bell again. This time, Bardo hid out of sight, which forced Schaeffer to step out of the apartment building's doorway. He jumped out and shot her point-blank in the chest. Schaeffer died while lying in the doorway of the apartment building.

After Bardo shot Schaeffer, he left the scene and boarded a bus for Arizona. Bardo's sister knew of his obsession with Schaeffer.

Robert Bardo, an obsessed fan who followed and killed actress Rebecca Schaeffer, appears in court after being charged with Schaeffer's murder. He was found guilty.

When she heard of the actress's murder, she called authorities in Los Angeles and turned her brother in. He was arrested when he got off the bus in Arizona. Bardo was convicted of first-degree murder and sentenced to life in prison without parole.

Schaeffer's murder was among the first highly publicized accounts of celebrity stalking, and it helped to implement anti-stalking legislation nationwide. Her murder became national news. She was a young, beautiful, rising television star who was murdered in a shocking, senseless way. Her death shined a light on stalking, and for the first time stalking victims had a voice in their fight to establish legal protections.

As a result of both Schaeffer's death and complaints of stalking and other threats voiced by a number of celebrities and public figures, then-governor of California George Deukmejian signed a law that prohibited the DMV from releasing addresses to unauthorized individuals, including detective agencies, and the Los Angeles Police Department created the Threat Management Team to directly address stalking complaints. California's antistalking law was passed in 1990, and by 1993, antistalking laws were in effect nationwide.

Stalking Is a Crime in All Fifty States

While all fifty states and the District of Columbia have stalking laws, statutes and definitions of stalking vary from state to state. Prosecuting a stalker can be a complicated endeavor because the individual acts of a stalker, on their own, may not amount to any type of criminal behavior. A rose left on a doorstep may seem like a non-threatening gesture. But to a stalking victim, it could be interpreted as an indication that her stalker knows where she lives. Context is critical to understanding if an action by one person toward another can be defined as stalking. The seriousness of a stalking act is defined by its designation as either a misdemeanor or a felony.

Misdemeanors are lesser criminal offenses that are punishable by up to a year in jail in most states. Other punishments include payment of a fine, probation, community service, restitution, or a combination of these punishments. Examples of misdemeanors are speeding, trespassing, or vandalism.

Felonies are the most serious type of criminal offenses and often involve serious physical harm or the threat of harm to a person.

U.S. Attorney General Eric Holder spoke at the first meeting of the National Advisory Committee on Violence Against Women. The committee's goal is to improve law enforcement's response to issues such as domestic violence, dating violence, sexual assault, and stalking.

Assault, battery, arson, rape, and murder are examples of felonies. If you are convicted of a felony, your punishment is time in prison. You can be sentenced to months, years, or life in prison. In states that have the death penalty, a jury could sentence you to death for your crime.

In the United States, thirty-five states classify stalking as a felony upon the second offense, or the second time a stalker commits a threatening act toward someone else. However, all states have different definitions of what constitutes a stalking crime. States define stalking as a crime based on the stalker's course of conduct. According to the U.S. Department of Justice, course of conduct is typically defined as one or more intentional acts that "evidence a continuity of purpose." All states have a different threshold for the number of acts that need to be committed to satisfy the definition of course of conduct for your state. For example, Ohio defines course of conduct as two or more actions or incidents closely related in time. In Louisiana, it's a series of acts over any amount of time that prove an intent to inflict emotional distress.

You Can Help Prove Stalking Intent

Each state recognizes the crime of stalking in one of two ways: as general intent or specific intent. For general intent, when a crime of stalking is being prosecuted in court, prosecutors do not have to prove the stalker intended the consequences of his or her actions. In states that categorize stalking as specific intent, prosecutors must prove that the stalker intended to cause the result of his or her actions, such as the victim's fear of injury or death, for stalking to be considered a crime.

You can help prove intent to police or law enforcement agencies by saving any evidence that you are being stalked. This evidence can help support your case should your stalker be arrested and charged with a crime. If you are being stalked, you should save the following:

- Text messages or voice-mails left on your phone
- Videos you or others may have taken that show the stalker and his or her behavior
- E-mails, letters, photos, cards, or unwanted items the stalker sent you
- Comments, threats, personal information, or other information the stalker posted about you online
- The details of any interaction you have had with the stalker, including the times, places, and dates of any and all incidents that occur, names and contact information of any witnesses, and a detailed account of what your stalker said to you or did

TRACK YOUR STALKER'S BEHAVIOR: HOW TO USE A BEHAVIOR LOG

Tracking your stalker's behavior is more than documenting evidence to show general intent or specific intent. It is also used to show course of conduct, consistency of behavior, and the types of behaviors and methods your stalker is using against you. A behavior log can help increase the credibility that the stalker's actions produced fear or intimidation and caused you to suffer physically, emotionally, or psychologically. The behavior log should include four key items:

(continued on the next page)

(continued from the previous page)

1. Incident description: Document the date, time, and specific description of each and every stalking incident, even if you aren't sure the incident is the work of your stalker. Sometimes stalkers use third parties to deliver messages, drop off packages, or commit acts that instill fear in their victims.

2. Corroborating evidence: All evidence should be preserved. Keep all correspondence, take screen shots of online harassment, save all gifts, take photos of text messages, and keep all recordings of voice-mail messages. Keep this list safe and private, and make sure it's accessible by only you or a trusted friend or relative.

3. Law enforcement notification: If you decide to call law enforcement to report a stalking incident, you should keep a record of the communication. Write down the date and time of the call and why you are calling; ask for the responding officer's name and badge number; document what the officer said to you and any action the officer took; and request a copy of the police report for your records.

4. Your state of mind/feelings: Write down how each incident made you feel or if you were forced to change your lifestyle in response to a particular stalking incident. Document your feelings about each incident and explain the content of the incident. Include past threats and behaviors that made this new incident seem more frightening or distressing.

Some states require a stalker's behavior to cause the victim actual fear, which usually requires the victim to testify in court about his or her feelings and/or how the stalker's behavior has

Musician Ashanti *(center)* arrives at the Manhattan District Attorney's Office to testify to a grand jury about her stalker, Devar Hurd.

caused the victim to change his or her lifestyle as a result of the stalking. Some states require actual fear from the victim as well as proof that a reasonable person would also feel fear. The level of fear necessary to prove a stalking crime varies by each state. Some states require that the victim feel terrorized, frightened, intimidated, or threatened that the stalker intends to injure him or her. Other states require that the victim fear serious bodily injury or death. Some states require that a victim have fear for his or her safety or suffer other emotional distress.

In addition, many states require that the stalker pose a credible threat to the victim. Some states require proof that the stalker is capable of carrying out his or her threats. Implicit threats, or those that may only be understood by the victim, are much harder to prove in stalking cases, especially among formerly intimate partners. Many states also need victims to prove that they are the target of a stalker's acts and that these acts pose an immediate danger to the victim. Other states extend the stalker's target to not just the victim but also to the victim's family, current partner, and even professional counselors or lawyers working with the victim.

CHAPTER 5

Getting Help

Stalking victims fear not knowing what will happen next. It's important to remember that being stalked is not your fault. You did not do anything to invite a stalker into your life, nor did you do anything to attract unwanted attention. Stalkers thrive on being in control and being in power. Their behaviors are unpredictable and can often become very dangerous.

Protect Yourself

Learn to take safety precautions that minimize a stalker's ability to learn information about you. Follow these general guidelines:

Do not personally respond to the stalker's attention. Don't even tell him or her to stop or to leave you alone. Some stalkers have mental health issues, and any reaction by you can be perceived as encouraging their behavior. Refrain from seeking retaliation or making counterthreats to your stalker.

Improve your home security. Get a security system, install outdoor lighting that comes on using motion sensors, and keep all doors and windows locked at all times. Remove any landscaping, such as trees and bushes, from around your home to

Emily Bills carries a rape whistle on her keychain as she gets out of her car at her home. Her friend was attacked in the alleyway next to Bills's apartment near the University of Colorado at Boulder.

eliminate places for your stalker to hide or watch you in your home.

Learn self-defense. Classes on self-defense are available at local martial arts facilities as well as some fitness centers. Consider carrying pepper spray, a whistle, or other items that can deter a stalker or attract help.

Always carry a cell phone on you, and inform family or friends if you will be going someplace alone, how long you will be, and when you expect to return. Keep a pen and paper in your car or in your purse so you can write down license plate numbers of cars you think might be following you.

Vary your daily routine. Leave for work or school at different times. Vary when you do regular weekly activities like grocery shopping and errands. Do your errands in a different part of town. Take different routes to and from places you visit often. Arrive home from work at different times.

Tell people about your stalker. Let family, friends, colleagues and/or classmates know what's going on. Inform security personnel at work and school that you have a stalker. Tell family and friends important information about your stalker, such as what kind of vehicle he or she drives, if you know his or her name, and his or her physical description.

Employ common security protocols: use caller ID before answering your phone; ask people to identify themselves before answering your door; and ask for identification from utility workers, phone company representatives, or workers you hire for work around your home.

CREATING A STALKING SAFETY PLAN

A stalking safety plan is a combination of suggestions, plans, and responses created to help victims reduce their risk of harm. It contains contingency plans, such as pre-established, safe places for a victim to go, as well as important phone numbers a victim may need.

For victims in immediate danger:
- Go to a local police station.
- Seek safety at a trusted friend or family member's home.
- Go to a domestic violence emergency shelter.
- Stay in a public area with a crowd until you can get help (stalkers are less likely to create a disturbance if people are around).

For victims in danger, but not immediately at risk:
- Get a protective order or restraining order.
- Educate yourself on your state's stalking laws.
- Document all stalking incidents.
- Have a contingency plan in place:

    • Memorize the phone numbers and locations of law enforcement agencies.
    • Memorize contact numbers for medical care, legal services, child care, family and friends, et cetera, for use after safety has been secured.

- Alert people who may be involved in your contingency plan, such as family, friends, law enforcement, school, and work.
- Install preventive measures such as a security system or doors with dead bolts, change all locks, vary travel routes, screen all calls, document all stalking incidents, and avoid going anywhere alone.
- Know where you can get additional help, such as domestic violence shelters, crisis hotlines and programs, prosecutor's offices, and law enforcement agencies.
- Limit or stop your use of all social media.

Avoid social media, or use strict privacy settings to allow only people you know to see your posts, photos, or status updates.

Prepare an emergency kit in the event you need to leave your home quickly. Include items such as a prepaid cell phone, clothing, extra money, and overnight items. Be aware that stalkers are skilled at getting information about you from other people, can hack computer systems to gain access to information, and may befriend people in your life to get close to you.

Where to Get Help

Deciding to get help is a personal decision you need to make for yourself, when you are ready. Local law enforcement agencies can assist you in determining if your stalker has committed

You can get help by contacting law enforcement and by filing a restraining order, or protective order, against your stalker.

a crime or if laws have been broken. They can also help you file a protective order, which legally limits your stalker from contacting you.

Sometimes called a restraining order, protection-from-abuse order, or peace order, a protective order is a judicial ruling that restricts a person's movements and activities. It can protect you from coming into contact with your stalker and prevents your stalker from communicating with you in any form. Under a protective order, your stalker cannot visit your house, call or text you, e-mail you, post online comments, or otherwise harass you without facing a criminal penalty such as arrest or serving time in jail.

If you sustained an injury caused by your stalker, you should seek immediate medical attention. Don't wait. Some injuries, such as internal bleeding, may not be felt until hours later. When they are apparent, they could be much more serious than if you sought medical attention sooner. If you do seek medical intervention, document all injuries diagnosed by your doctor and keep all information regarding treatment. This information may be useful at a later date should you seek a protective order or need to present evidence in court.

If you are living in a constant state of fear, a counselor or therapist may be able to help you deal with the emotions you may be experiencing. It's not uncommon for a stalking victim to feel a wide range of emotions, from helpless and fearful to empowered and determined. Understanding your feelings and how best to manage them during this ordeal can assist in helping you make smart, safe choices in how to handle your stalker. Hotlines, group counseling, and individual counseling can provide you with insight on your feelings and help you understand the mind of a stalker and his or her motivations.

Stalkers want to isolate you. Stay connected with friends and family, and avoid going anywhere alone. If you know someone is being stalked, offer your support and friendship.

Helping a Friend

If you know someone who is being stalked, support her during this difficult time. Don't blame the victim, and refrain from suggesting that she brought the stalking on by her choices or actions. Educate yourself about stalking, and be there for your friend.

You may feel compelled to suggest things your friend should do, such as contact law enforcement authorities, call a crisis hotline, seek therapy, or other actions. Every stalking scenario is different, and victims must decide for themselves when and how they want to handle it.

Many stalkers try to isolate their victims from family and friends. Be patient and offer your continued support. Check in on your friend and offer to accompany him or her to school or on outings. Most important, avoid getting involved with the stalker. It's normal to want to defend and protect your friends, but getting involved could put you in danger. A stalker could view you as a threat to his or her relationship with the victim. You could also become the stalker's target for trying to help your friend.

Moving On

You can reclaim your life and live without fear of what a stalker will do. Whether your stalker has been convicted of a crime and is serving time in prison, or he or she is still actively engaged in stalking you, you can move on and regain a sense of control in your life.

Join a stalking victims' support group. These supportive communities can help you learn from other stalking victims how they survived and moved on. Plus, sharing your story with others who have had the same experiences can be empowering and offer some encouragement.

Consider moving to a new town. It may be an extreme reaction, but if your stalker is persistent and you are unable to secure any legal protections, it could be your only option. In a new town you can create a new life and reestablish some safety away from your stalker. If you choose to move, avoid making announcements on social media, tell only trusted people where you are going, and give your contact information to very few people to avoid any chance of your stalker learning your whereabouts.

Seek professional help through a counselor or therapist to help you deal with your feelings of fear and help you build up your confidence to begin living a full life again. A therapist can offer

You can move on after being stalked. Reconnect with friends, seek support from family, join a support group, and return to your normal activities as soon as you can.

insights into your situation and offer you ways to manage your feelings. He or she can also be a trusted person to confide in.

You will be able to build a life again and engage in the greater community without fear of your stalker. By creating a secure life, making smart decisions about being proactive about your personal protection, and by using the resources available to you via law enforcement and other local and national agencies, you can move forward with a sense of security, confidence, and strength as you rebuild your life and reestablish your personal freedom independent of the stalking incidents that may have defined your life.

GLOSSARY

ANXIETY Fear or nervousness about what might happen.

BENIGN Not causing harm or damage.

CORROBORATE To support or help prove by providing information or evidence.

DELUSIONAL Having a false idea or belief that is caused by mental illness.

FELONY A crime for which the punishment by federal law may be death or imprisonment for more than one year.

FINE A monetary sum imposed as punishment for an offense.

INSOMNIA An ongoing inability to get enough sleep.

MISDEMEANOR A crime that is less serious than a felony.

PREMEDITATED Describing an action taken with intent, forethought, and planning.

PROBATION A period of time in which a person who has committed a crime or has done something bad is allowed to stay out of prison if that person behaves well and does not commit another crime.

PROSECUTOR A lawyer who represents the side in a court case that accuses a person of a crime and who tries to prove that the person is guilty.

RECIDIVISM A tendency to return to a previous behavior, usually used in reference to criminal acts.

RESTITUTION Payment that is made to someone for damage or trouble.

SURVEILLANCE The act of carefully watching someone or something.

THRESHOLD The point or level at which something begins or changes.

TRESPASSING The crime of going on someone's land without permission.

TUMULTUOUS Involving a lot of violence, confusion, or disorder.

VANDALISM The act of deliberately destroying or damaging property.

VOYEURISM The act of seeing, talking, or writing about something that is considered to be private.

WILLFUL Done deliberately.

FOR MORE INFORMATION

Break the Cycle
P.O. Box 66165
Washington, DC 20035
(202) 824-0707
Website: http://www.breakthecycle.org
Break the Cycle is a nonprofit organization that provides dating
    abuse prevention programs for young people to help them
    prevent and escape unhealthy relationships. The organiza-
    tion also promotes laws and policies that protect victims of
    dating abuse.

The DATE SAFE Project
P.O. Box 20906
Greenfield, WI 53220-0906
(920) 326-3687
Website: http://www.datesafeproject.org
The DATE SAFE Project teaches young people how to address
    issues such as verbal consent, respecting of boundaries,
    sexual decision making, and bystander intervention.

Hardy Girls, Healthy Women
P.O. Box 821
Waterville, ME 04903-0821
(207) 861-8131
Website: http://www.hghw.org
Hardy Girls, Healthy Women is a nonprofit organization that
    supports girls and women and focuses particularly on how
    they are affected by relationships and social systems. Its
    goal "is that all girls and women experience equality, inde-
    pendence, and safety in their everyday lives."

National Center for Victims of Crimes
2000 M Street NW, Suite 480
Washington, DC 20036
(202) 467-8700
Website: http://www.victimsofcrime.org
The National Center for Victims of Crimes works with local,
    state, and federal partners to advocate for stronger
    rights, protections, and services for crime victims; pro-
    vides educational services, training, and evaluation of
    programs; and is a trusted resource for information for
    victims of crimes.

National Online Resource Center for Violence Against Women
3605 Vartan Way, Suite 101
Harrisburg, PA 17110
(800) 537-2238
Website: http://www.vawnet.org
On VAWnet, the National Online Resource Center for Violence
    Against Women hosts an online collection of resources on
    domestic violence, sexual violence, and related issues.

National Organization for Victim Assistance (NOVA)
510 King Street, Suite 424
Alexandria, VA 22314
(703) 535-6682
Website: https://www.trynova.org
NOVA was founded in 1975, making it the oldest national orga-
    nization for victim assistance in the United States. Its
    mission "is to champion dignity and compassion for those
    harmed by crime and crisis."

Stalking Resource Center

2000 M Street NW, Suite 480

Washington, DC 20036

(202) 467-8700

Website: http://www.victimsofcrime.org/our-programs/
stalking-resource-center

The Stalking Resource Center was founded in 2000 as a part-
nership of the National Center for Victims of Crime and the
U.S. Department of Justice Office on Violence Against
Women. The center has trained over one hundred thousand
professionals to work with victims and help hundreds of
communities address stalking.

Websites

Because of the changing nature of Internet links, Rosen
Publishing has developed an online list of websites related to
the subject of this book. This site is updated regularly. Please
use this link to access this list:

http://www.rosenlinks.com/CVAW/Stalk

Becker, Gavin de. *The Gift of Fear and Other Survival Signals that Protect Us from Violence.* New York, NY: Dell Publishing, 1999.

Brennan, Kate. *In His Sights: One Woman's Stalking Nightmare.* New York, NY: Harper Perennial, 2009.

Chatting with Kids About Being Online. Damascus, MD: Penny Hill Press Inc., 2014.

Clarkson, Polly. *Stalkers: Disturbing True-Life Stories of Harassment, Jealousy, and Obsession.* London, England: John Blake Publishing, 2007.

Cohen Wood, Tyler. *Catching the Catfishers: Disarm the Online Pretenders, Predators, and Perpetrators Who Are Out to Ruin Your Life.* Pompton Plains, NJ: Career Press, 2014.

Coleman Carter, Toni L. *When Trouble Finds You: Overcoming Child Abuse, Teen Pregnancy, Domestic Violence and Discovering the Remarkable Power of the Human Spirit.* Highland Park, IL: RTC Publishing, 2013.

Eastham, Chad. *The Truth About Dating, Love & Just Being Friends.* Nashville, TN: Thomas Nelson/HarperCollins Christian Publishing, 2011.

Fairweather, Lynn. *Stop Signs: Recognizing, Avoiding, and Escaping Abusive Relationships.* Berkeley, CA: Seal Press, 2012.

Hitchcock, J.A. *True Crime Online: Shocking Stories of Scamming, Stalking, Murder, and Mayhem.* Medford, NJ: Information Today, Inc., 2012.

Lawton, Sandra Augustyn. *Abuse and Violence Information for Teens: Health Tips About the Causes and*

Consequences of Abusive and Violent Behavior. Detroit, MI: Omnigraphics, Inc., 2007.

Levy, Barrie. *In Love and in Danger: A Teen's Guide to Breaking Free of Abusive Relationships.* Berkeley, CA: Seal Press, 2006.

Moore, Alexis. *Cyber Self-Defense: Expert Advice to Avoid Online Predators, Identity Theft, and Cyberbullying.* Guilford, CT: Lyons Press, 2014.

Archer, Dale. "Reading Between the (Head)Lines."
   Psychology Today, March 11, 2013. Retrieved November
   6, 2014 (http://www.psychologytoday.com/blog/reading
   -between-the-headlines/201303/is-jodi-arias-sociopath).

Axthelm, Pete. "An Innocent Life, a Heartbreaking Death."
   People, July 31, 1989. Retrieved November 5, 2014
   (http://www.people.com/people/archive/article/
   0,,20120867,00.html).

Kiefer, Michael. "Arias Saga: A Sordid Affair Turns Deadly."
   USA Today, May 9, 2013. Retrieved November 7, 2014
   (http://www.usatoday.com/story/news/nation/2013/
   05/09/jodi-arias-trial-saga/2146249/).

Loveisrespect.org. "5 Stalking Myths Debunked." January 9,
   2012. Retrieved November 14, 2014 (http://www
   .loveisrespect.org/5-stalking-myths-debunked).

McKinley Jr., James C. "Mistrial Declared for Man Accused
   of Stalking R&B Star Ashanti." New York Times,
   December 18, 2014. Retrieved April 2, 2015 (http://www.
   nytimes.com/2014/12/19/nyregion/mistrial-declared-for-
   man-accused-of-stalking-rb-star-ashanti.
   html?ref=topics&_r=0).

Moore, Alexis A. "How Cyberstalkers Obtain Your Personal
   Data." Retrieved April 2, 2015 (http://womensissues.about.
   com/od/violenceagainstwomen/a/CyberPersonalIn.htm).

Moore, Alexis A. "'I Was a Victim of Cyberstalking:' One
   Woman's Story." Retrieved April 2, 2015 (http://
   womensissues.about.com/od/violenceagainstwomen/
   a/CyberstalkStory.htm).

National Center for Victims of Crime. "Stalking Fact Sheet."
   Retrieved November 27, 2014 (http://www

.victimsofcrime.org/docs/src/stalking-fact-sheet_english
.pdf?sfvrsn=4).

Network of Victim Assistance. "Stalking." Retrieved
November 5, 2014 (http://www.novabucks.org/
otherinformation/stalking).

Newman, Andy. "Stalked: A Decade on the Run." *New York
Times*, July 31, 2008. Retrieved November 22, 2014
(http://www.nytimes.com/2008/07/31/fashion/31stalk.
html?pagewanted=all&_r=0).

Nightlionsecurity.com. "5 Privacy Tips to Avoid Being
Stalked on Social Media." Retrieved November 6,
2014 (https://www.nightlionsecurity.com/blog/privacy
/2014/04/5-privacy-tips-avoid-stalked-social-media).

Ramsland, Katherine. "Stalkers: The Psychological Terrorist."
Retrieved November 20, 2014 (http://www.crimelibrary
.com/criminal_mind/psychology/stalkers/1.html).

Schlikerman, Becky. "Streamwood Teen Who Was Stalked
Takes Her Story to Washington." *Chicago Tribune*,
January 18, 2011. Retrieved November 5, 2014 (http://
articles.chicagotribune.com/2011-01-18/news/ct
-met-childhood-stalker-20110118_1_new-laws
-streamwood-police).

Serpe, Gina. "Shawn Johnson's Sanity-Challenged Stalker
Gets Five Years in Mental Ward." EOnline, July 13, 2010.
Retrieved November 27, 2014 (http://www.eonline.com/
news/190096/shawn-johnson-s-sanity-challenged
-stalker-gets-five-years-in-mental-ward).

Shahani, Aarti. "Smartphones Are Used To Stalk, Control
Domestic Abuse Victims." *NPR*, September 15, 2014.
Retrieved November 4, 2014 (http://www.npr.org/blogs/

alltechconsidered/2014/09/15/346149979/smartphones
-are-used-to-stalk-control-domestic-abuse-victims).

Van der Zande, Irene. "Stalking: How to Protect Yourself."
Retrieved November 30, 2014 (http://www.kidpower
.org/library/article/stalking).

Vojtech, Jim, Lee Ferran, and Clayton Sandell. "Shawn
Johnson Exclusive: 'I Had to Stand Up' to Stalker." *Good
Morning America*, June 22, 2010. Retrieved November 27,
2014 (http://abcnews.go.com/GMA/shawn-johnson
-stalker-stand/story?id=10976311).

Women's Self-Defense Institute. "The Stalker: Understanding
the Five Different Types." Retrieved November 5, 2014
(http://www.self-defense-mind-body-spirit.com/
stalker.html).

INDEX

About the Author

Laura La Bella is the author of many nonfiction children's books. She has profiled actress and activist Angelina Jolie in *Angelina Jolie: Goodwill Ambassador to the UN*; reported on the declining availability of the world's fresh water supply in *Not Enough to Drink: Pollution, Drought, and Tainted Water Supplies*; and examined the food industry in *Safety and the Food Supply*. La Bella lives in Rochester, New York, with her husband and two sons.

Photo Credits